CROSSWORD AMERICA

AMERICAN HISTORY TO 1900

Written by Cathryn J. Long

Illustrations by Larry Nolte

LOWELL HOUSE JUVENILE

LOS ANGELES

CONTEMPORARY BOOKS

CHICAGO

Publisher: Jack Artenstein
Director of Publishing Services: Rena Copperman
Editorial Director, Juvenile: Brenda Pope-Ostrow
Director of Juvenile Development: Amy Downing
Director of Art Production: Bret Perry

Library of Congress Catalog Card Number: 97-76092

ISBN: 1-56565-934-1

Lowell House books can be purchased at special discounts when ordered in bulk for premiums and special sales.
Contact Department TC at the following address:

Lowell House Juvenile
2020 Avenue of the Stars, Suite 300
Los Angeles, CA 90067

PHOTO CREDITS:
On the cover, the George Washington photo is courtesy of the National Archives;
the drummer boys photo is courtesy of the Library of Congress.
On pages 19, 21, 37, 39, 57, and 59, the photos are courtesy of
the Library of Congress. On page 23, the photo is
courtesy of the National Archives.

Manufactured in the United States of America

10 9 8 7 6 5 4 3 2

CONTENTS

To the Teacher and Parent

The crossword puzzles in this book are a practical and fun review of U.S. history, from the days of its first inhabitants up to the twentieth century. You can use these puzzles to introduce a history topic, or to review one. They provide an alternative way of learning that reinforces textbook work. Students can do the puzzles individually or in small groups. Because the puzzles emphasize reading comprehension, vocabulary, and spelling, they have a place in language arts teaching, too. Home teachers and teachers of English as a Second Language may also find the puzzles useful.

To find the clues and complete each puzzle, students will need to *read and understand* the introductory paragraphs, as well as *locate information in illustrations or maps* that accompany each puzzle. Students can also *locate an appropriate word on the alphabetical list of words* provided with each puzzle as another aid in solving the puzzle. If your students are unfamiliar with this type of puzzle, review with them the word numbering system and the way "across" words give clues for "down" words, and vice versa.

If you have already taught the topic that is featured for a puzzle, you may want to challenge students to complete as much of the puzzle as they can without reading the introduction, looking at the illustrations, or using the word list.

Each puzzle focuses on a specific topic, and the topics are arranged in six chronological and thematic units. Of course, not every history topic could be covered, but we have included those that are most often taught, and some that are simply most interesting and enjoyable. If a topic you teach is not included, you may want students to create their own crossword puzzles—complete with clues—and exchange them with one another.

For the Puzzle Player
(Students or anyone else interested in American history!)

D id you know that a hazard of living on the frontier was having snakes fall from the ceiling? Have you heard of the Wizard of Menlo Park? Did you know teddy bears were named for a president? This book will help you review these and many other U.S. history facts by solving crossword puzzles. All the clues you need to solve each puzzle are included with it. There are three ways to find clues:

1. Read the topic summary.
2. Look carefully at the pictures or maps that go with the puzzle.
3. Look for the right word in the puzzle word list.

The topics in this book are in chronological order, but you can solve each puzzle in any order you wish. Have fun learning about this amazing country in *Crossword America*!

NATIVES OF NORTH AMERICA

The first people to live in America came from Asia. Many thousands of years ago, during the Ice Age, a land bridge connected Asia to North America (where Alaska is today). Hunters most likely followed herds of large animals such as the elephantlike woolly mammoth across the land bridge. In time, groups of people were living across North and South America. These people are called natives because they were the first to live there.

At first, all Native Americans survived by hunting and gathering plant foods. Later, some discovered they could save seeds from these foods and plant them to grow more. In Mexico, native people first grew corn. After that, farming became very important to many tribes.

The Native American way of life depended on the area where each tribe lived. In North America east of the Mississippi River, Eastern Woodlands people hunted deer and used logs and bark to build homes and fences. On the Great Plains between the Mississippi River and the Rocky Mountains, buffalo were a source of food, clothing, and shelter. Buffalo hunting became easier for these tribes when Native Americans first got horses from the Spanish in the 1600s. Great Plains people made everything from tepees to bone tools from parts of the buffalo.

Northwest Coast people were rich: They had plentiful foods like salmon and resources like timber. These people thought it was a sign of strength and dignity to give away food and presents in big celebrations called potlatches. In the Southwest, natives grew corn and often lived in pueblos—apartment houses made of adobe (clay and straw bricks).

Most tribes had a chief—a wise man who helped the people make decisions. The shaman (SHAH-mun) was the tribe's spiritual leader and healer. Many members of the tribe helped educate the children through stories and rituals. These traditions remain among many Native American tribes today.

The first Europeans to reach America called the natives Indians. That was because they thought they had come to some Asian islands called the Indies! Even though the name was given by mistake, it stuck. Today, some Native Americans prefer to be called Indians.

Across

1. Northwest Native American celebration in which gifts and food are given away
6. In the Eastern _____, deer hunting was important.
7. This animal helped feed, clothe, and shelter Plains Indians.
8. A Native American spiritual leader

10. An apartment building created by Southwest Native Americans
11. Continent from which people first came to America
12. Native American children listened to these as part of their education.
14. People who first called Native Americans "Indians"
15. An important farm crop for native people

*Foods Native
Americans first grew*

Down

1. We make french fries from this vegetable, grown by Native Americans.
2. Term for a Native American leader
3. For thousands of years, the first Americans continued to hunt game and _____ plant foods.
4. Material from which pueblos are built
5. Fish that helped make Northwest people wealthy
7. The first Americans came from Asia on a land _____.
9. An elephantlike animal hunted in the Ice Age
10. Horses changed the lives of people living in this area.
13. The name given to Native Americans by mistake

Land bridge, connecting Asia to North America

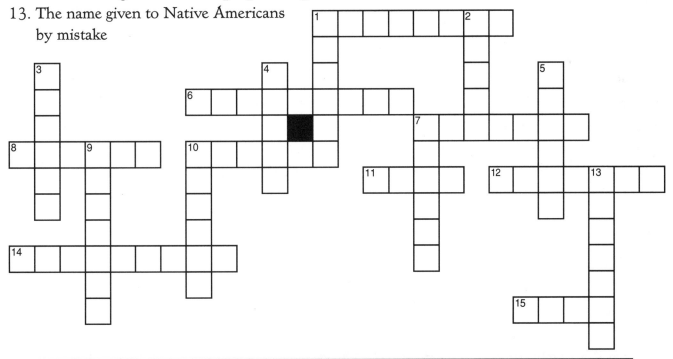

Word List

adobe	buffalo	gather	potato	shaman
Asia	chief	Indians	potlatch	stories
bridge	corn	mammoth	pueblo	Woodlands
	Europeans	plains	salmon	

EUROPEAN EXPLORERS

About a thousand years ago, Viking tales told of Vinland, a mysterious country across the sea. Leif Eriksson led Viking boats from Greenland to find Vinland. They arrived at the North American coast and settled briefly on the island now called Newfoundland.

Most of Europe, however, had not heard about the Viking adventure. Leaders of the strongest nations were trying to find a good way to reach Asia, where valuable silks and spices were traded. The Portuguese found a route by sea around southern Africa in the 1400s. But Christopher Columbus thought he could reach Asia by sailing west. Columbus looked for royal backing; he got it from Ferdinand and Isabella, monarchs of Spain. Even though he actually had found America, and made four voyages there, Columbus continued to believe it was Asia to his dying day.

Spanish and Portuguese explorers helped draw a true map of the world. Vasco Núñez de Balboa crossed Central America and found the Pacific Ocean on the other side. He claimed all the land bordering the ocean for Spain. Ferdinand Magellan's ships sailed all the way around the world. Soon, Spanish expeditions found gold and silver in Central and South America and claimed the land. But it was an Italian explorer, Amerigo Vespucci, whose name was used for the new continents.

Spanish treasure seekers also explored North America. Hernando de Soto failed to find riches in the Southeast. Francisco Vásquez de Coronado searched the Southwest for gold but found none. Juan Rodríguez Cabrillo claimed the land of California for Spain.

Along the East Coast, French and British explorers such as Henry Hudson, John Cabot, and Jacques Cartier looked for a water route, which some called the Northwest Passage. This waterway supposedly led from the north Atlantic to the riches of Asia. Though they never found it, they made land claims that became the foundation of Canada and the United States.

Across

2. Initials of the state now on the land Cabrillo claimed for Spain
4. Last name of the Viking explorer who first reached America
7. Name of an explorer who worked for England and Holland
9. His ships were the first to go around the world.
11. Number of trips to the New World made by Columbus
12. Cabrillo and Balboa claimed land bordering this ocean for Spain.
14. Viking name for Newfoundland
16. The explorer America is named for (his first name)
17. The country that claimed most of South and Central America

Northern European Explorers

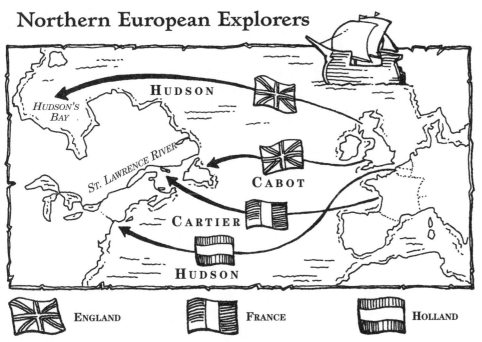

Down

1. The Spanish failed to find gold in _____ America.
2. This Spaniard explored the Southwest.
3. The explorer who tried to reach Asia by sailing west
5. The Spanish queen who backed Columbus's voyage
6. This man found that the Pacific lay on the other side of America.

8. A French explorer who entered the St. Lawrence River
10. The Portuguese reached Asia by sailing around this continent.
13. Columbus sought help from people who wore this.
15. Initials of a passage between the Atlantic and Pacific sought by French and British explorers

Word List

Africa	CA	crown	Isabella	Pacific
Amerigo	Cartier	Eriksson	Magellan	Spain
Balboa	Columbus	four	North	Vinland
	Coronado	Hudson	NW	

COLONIAL LIFE

English settlers began to arrive in North America in the early 1600s. They came for many reasons, though most hoped to become richer than they were in Europe. The gentlemen who founded the first permanent English colony, at Jamestown, Virginia, thought they would find gold lying on the ground. They had no such luck, and many of the settlers died before the colony finally made a profit from growing tobacco. Later arrivals on the East Coast found farming and trading were the best ways to gain prosperity.

Other settlers came to escape certain laws and rulers. For instance, the Pilgrims, who founded Plymouth, disagreed with the Church of England. They wanted a simpler church in which worshippers had a say. To them, the right to worship in their own way was worth the hardships they might find in the new land.

Along the Atlantic coast, colonies began as small settlements and, in time, were organized into large areas like the states we know today. The northeastern colonies, called New England, were home to a way of life brought by the Pilgrims and by the Puritans who founded Boston. Work, church, and education were important, and male church members could vote in town meetings. Shipbuilding and trade helped New Englanders make money. New England traders first organized the triangular trade in which rum was exchanged for slaves, who were exchanged in the Caribbean islands for molasses (made from the sugar cane grown there). The molasses was in turn brought to New England to be made into rum.

The middle colonies included New York, New Jersey, Delaware, and Pennsylvania. William Penn, an English Quaker, advertised religious freedom and good farmland in the colony he founded, Pennsylvania (meaning "Penn's Woods"). Huge crops of wheat were milled into flour and shipped out of Philadelphia, the capital. New settlers and lively business helped make Philadelphia the largest city in the colonies. New York also grew fast as a trade city.

To the south, in the coastal Tidewater region, large crops of rice, indigo (a blue dye), and tobacco grew well because of the climate. Africans were forced to work as slaves on the region's large farms, called plantations.

Across

1. The product that saved the Jamestown colony
3. Name of the first permanent English colony
6. Pennsylvania means "Penn's _____."
7. Part of the southern coast with large plantations
9. New Englanders governed themselves through town _____.
12. The colonists who founded Plymouth

14. What New Englanders valued most, along with work and church
15. The largest city in the English colonies
16. The product made into rum as part of the triangular trade

Down

1. New York grew because of this.
2. The Pilgrims wanted the right to do this in their own way.
4. Term for the trade in which molasses, made into rum, was exchanged for slaves

The Triangular Trade

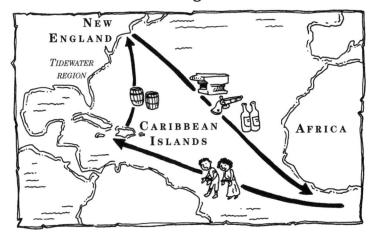

5. This word was often put before Old World place names to create new ones for the colonies, as in ___ England.
6. Labor; something New Englanders especially valued
8. The Pilgrims came to America to escape the rules of the _____ of England.
10. Africans forced to work on plantations
11. Blue dye plant grown on colonial plantations
13. Molasses for the triangular trade was produced in the West _____.

Word List

Church	indigo	New	Tidewater	Woods
education	Jamestown	Philadelphia	tobacco	work
Indies	meetings	Pilgrims	trade	worship
	molasses	slaves	triangular	

THE SPANISH SOUTHWEST

In some parts of the United States, the colonial past is Spanish instead of English. That is because Spain had an early claim on parts of North America. The oldest European-founded city in the United States is Spanish: St. Augustine, Florida, which dates from 1565. Most Spanish lands were in the Southwest. Spain ruled areas that are now part of Texas, Arizona, New Mexico, Nevada, Utah, Colorado, and California. The United States won or bought these lands piece by piece during the 1800s.

Missionaries were the pioneers of Spanish America. A mission was a church and settlement surrounded by its own farms and orchards where Native Americans were taught Christianity by Catholic priests. Native people worked at mission farms for little or no pay. To keep order, soldiers were often stationed near the mission at a fort called a presidio. In California, Father Junípero Serra founded a string of missions along the coast. Later, many of them helped form the beginnings of California cities, including Los Angeles and San Francisco.

Santa Fe ("Holy Faith"), today the capital of the state of New Mexico, was once the capital of Spain's northern territories. Spanish ranch owners brought the first cattle, sheep, and horses to the area. Stray horses, called mustangs, formed wild herds that roamed far distances. Spanish farmers also introduced orchard crops, such as oranges, olives, and peaches. Some Native Americans grew tired of Spanish rule. A Tewa Indian leader named Pope (poh-PAY) led a rebellion in 1680 that drove the Spanish out of the area we now call New Mexico for several years.

Across

1. A settlement where the Spanish taught their religion to the natives
3. Animals brought by the Spanish; their wool was used to weave blankets
4. State that was part of the Spanish southwest along with Texas, New Mexico, Nevada, Utah, Colorado, and California
10. California city that was once a mission: Los _____
12. Native Americans were expected to work for the Spanish for little or none of this.
14. The religion taught at Spanish missions
15. Spanish soldiers were posted here, near a mission or town.
16. Abbreviation for southwest
17. Name of the Tewa leader who rebelled against the Spanish

A Few Words from the Spanish

TORNADO

RANCH

PATIO

MUSTANG

CORRAL

Down

1. Term, which originated in Spain, for a wild horse
2. Area where Pope rebelled: ___ Mexico
5. The oldest European-founded city in the U.S.: St. _____
6. Second word in the name of the capital of the Spanish southwest
7. State on the Atlantic coast that once belonged to Spain
8. Area with fruit trees, introduced by the Spanish
9. Spanish term Americans use for a paved outdoor area on the grounds of a house
11. Last name of the man who founded California's coastal Spanish missions
13. Catholic who taught Native Americans at Spanish missions

Word List

Angeles	Christianity	mustang	pay	Serra
Arizona	Fe	New	Pope	sheep
Augustine	Florida	orchard	presidio	SW
	mission	patio	priest	

INDIANS AND SETTLERS

When Europeans and Native Americans first met, they were often friendly. Columbus exchanged gifts with the Arawak (AHR-uh-wok) people when he landed on the Caribbean island of Hispaniola (hiss-pah-NYO-luh). A Native American named Squanto helped the Pilgrims survive by teaching them to plant corn and showing them ways to catch fish. At Jamestown, a group of tribes led by Chief Powhatan (pow-HAH-tuhn) gave corn to the starving colonists.

Quickly, however, conflict became the rule between settlers and Indians. The settlers tried to buy land, or they simply took it. Most Indians thought land could not be bought or sold but belonged to those who were using it at the moment. As settlers built and farmed farther west, Indians fought them, raiding villages and farms. Settlers also raided Indian settlements. At times, the conflict became real war. One example is King Philip's War, in which the son of a chief who had welcomed the Pilgrims fought New Englanders.

A greater conflict between Indians and English settlers began in the mid 1700s. The French were fighting the British in a war in Europe. At the time, French traders were buying furs from American Indians in territory north and west of the English colonies. France claimed that territory, as did Britain. The European war spread to North America, where it was called the French and Indian War. Many Indians joined the French in fighting the British. The British won the war in 1763, but they agreed to keep settlers east of the Appalachian Mountains.

The American Revolution put an end to the British agreement, and settlers began moving west. The Shawnee leader Tecumseh (teh-CUM-seh) desperately tried to keep back the tide of settlement. He tried to unite all the tribes west of the Appalachians to stop the settlement. He did not succeed, and the tribes were pushed farther westward.

The greatest European weapon against the Indians turned out to be disease. Some historians think as many as two-thirds of all Native Americans in North America were killed by European diseases such as smallpox and the flu.

Across

1. After 1863, England agreed to keep settlers east of these mountains.
4. Settlers and Indians would often ____ each other's settlements.
6. A European disease that killed many Indians
7. Name of the people who were on the island where Columbus landed
9. Item traded by Indians to the French for manufactured goods
11. Most Indians did not think it possible to buy or _____ land.

13. Shawnee chief who tried to unite many tribes
14. Indian who helped the Pilgrims survive
16. Name of the chief who helped save Jamestown from starvation
17. Nationality of settlers fighting the French and Indians

Down

Fur Trade

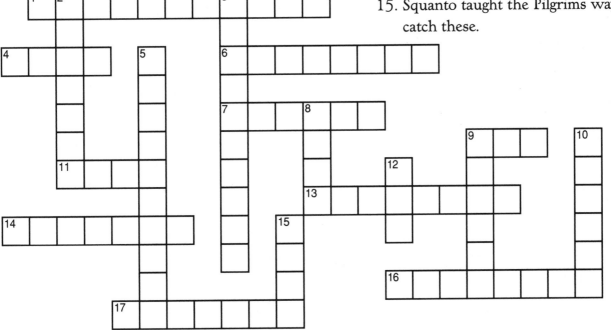

2. King _____ War was fought in New England between settlers and Indians.
3. Name of the island where Columbus exchanged gifts with Indians
5. After this war, settlers poured westward across the Appalachians: the American _____.
8. Direction in which Indians were often forced to move
9. These people were trading partners with Indians.
10. France fought English colonists in the French and _____ War.
12. Indians often got this weapon in exchange for furs.
15. Squanto taught the Pilgrims ways to catch these.

Word List

Appalachian	fish	Hispaniola	raid	Squanto
Arawak	French	Indian	Revolution	Tecumseh
English	fur	Philip's	sell	west
	gun	Powhatan	smallpox	

THE COLONISTS PROTEST

In 1765, the British government decided to tax the thirteen English colonies to help pay for the French and Indian War. The government ordered a stamp tax. This tax required colonists to pay to get a stamp on newspapers, calendars, and every sort of public paper. People were upset at having to pay the tax, but they were even more disturbed by the way the government had created the tax. Every colony had an elected assembly led by a governor. Normally, colonial money matters were decided by the assembly in each colony. But this time, no assembly had been allowed to help decide. Angry assembly members, such as Patrick Henry, protested in every colony.

The British, surprised by this outcry, decided to take back, or repeal, the law that created the stamp tax. However, they soon passed the Townshend Acts, which taxed many goods such as cloth, glass, and tea sent from England to the colonies.

Colonists, especially in Boston, objected. Anger grew when British soldiers shot several protesting colonists in what was named the Boston Massacre. Samuel Adams led a secret society of colonial men called the Sons of Liberty in anti-British acts. Disguised as Indians, the Sons of Liberty threw tea off a British ship into the harbor water. This event became known as the Boston Tea Party.

Neighbors divided depending on their view of England. Loyalist Tories were supporters of the British government, and Patriots protested against it. As war threatened, many Tories left the colonies and moved north to Canada. Some who remained in the colonies were covered with hot tar and feathers by unruly Patriots.

The colonies drew together under the British threat. In 1774, they organized the first Continental Congress, with delegates from all the colonies (except, at first, Georgia). As the Revolutionary War began, this congress served as the first form of American government.

Across

3. When the Townshend Acts were passed, colonial women wove more of their own _____.
4. Incident in which British soldiers shot several colonists; called the Boston _____
8. Name of British acts taxing goods sent to the colonies
9. Number of British colonies in America
13. Colonists in favor of the British government
14. Men dumped tea in the harbor at the Boston Tea _____.
15. Many Tories fled to this country.
16. Last name of the leader of protests in Boston
17. Colonists had to pay for one of these on all public papers.

Down

1. City at the center of colonial protests
2. Colonial official who led elected assembly in each colony
5. Each colony elected members of this group.
6. The _____ Congress spoke for all the colonies.
7. Some Tories were covered with hot tar and these.
8. Colonists did not want to pay this.
10. To take back; what the British did with the stamp tax
11. Popular beverage taxed by the British
12. The British created taxes to pay for this.
14. Initials of a patriot who spoke against the stamp tax

Boston Tea Party

Word List

Adams	cloth	Massacre	stamp	Tories
assembly	Continental	Party	tax	Townshend
Boston	feathers	PH	tea	war
Canada	governor	repeal	thirteen	

THE REVOLUTIONARY WAR

On April 18, 1775, Paul Revere rode hard along the road from Boston to the nearby towns of Lexington and Concord. His job was to warn people that British soldiers were coming to take the colonists' ammunition and to arrest Patriot leaders. Local "minutemen," farmers who had trained as Patriot soldiers, were prepared for the announcement. As the British approached the towns, the minutemen turned out to exchange fire. These were the first shots of the Revolutionary War.

The Continental Congress met in Philadelphia and decided to ask Britain's King George for peace. But they also decided to prepare for possible all-out war. They hired George Washington, formerly an army officer under the British, to lead a Continental army. At their first full battle, called the Battle of Bunker Hill, Patriot soldiers fought well—but their ammunition ran out and they were defeated.

Even as the army went into action, many colonists remained doubtful about rebelling. In 1776, a pamphlet by Thomas Paine called *Common Sense* helped colonists decide that independence from England was the best idea. The Continental Congress approved a Declaration of Independence on July 4, 1776. That day, the United States of America was born.

The Revolutionary War was hard-fought. Washington was responsible for pulling the army together and training them. Yet the men had to fight not only the well-trained and -supplied British but also German soldiers called Hessians. King George of England hired the Hessians to help him win the war.

Washington led his army across the Delaware River to surprise the Hessians with a victory at Trenton, New Jersey. Another major win at Saratoga helped convince the French to enter the war on the side of the new United States. In spite of the help, the Continental army suffered a long, cold winter at Valley Forge when the British took over Philadelphia.

After many more battles, the Americans and French trapped the British at Yorktown, Virginia, in 1781 and won the war.

Across

5. The allies who joined the United States to fight the British
8. When the Continental army won this battle, the French decided to enter the war as American allies.
10. Shots at Lexington and Concord are considered the first of the Revolutionary _____.
11. Last name of the messenger who warned people between Boston and Lexington
13. She was called Molly _____ because she brought water to thirsty soldiers.
15. Name given to men trained to fight the British at a moment's notice

16. Term for a hired German soldier in the Revolutionary War
17. Location of the final battle of the Revolution

Down

1. River crossed by Washington and his men to get to Trenton
2. Paul Revere warned people that the _____ were coming.
3. An early Boston battle was named after this hill.

Some Heroes of the Revolution

Mary McCauley, nicknamed "Molly Pitcher," brought soldiers water and loaded cannons.

Francis Marion, the "Swamp Fox," raided the British in the Carolinas.

4. In 1776, the Continental Congress issued the _____ of Independence.
6. Washington's army surprised the Hessians at this city.
7. Last name of the American officer nicknamed the "Swamp Fox"
9. Name of the king of England at the time of the Revolution
12. Where Washington's army spent a long, cold winter: _____ Forge
14. Last name of the author of *Common Sense*

Word List

British	Delaware	Marion	Pitcher	Valley
Bunker	French	minutemen	Revere	War
Declaration	George	Paine	Saratoga	Yorktown
	Hessian		Trenton	

THOMAS JEFFERSON

Born on a Virginia plantation, Thomas Jefferson was well educated at the College of William and Mary in Williamsburg. He was good at many things, including languages, music, writing, and architecture, but he decided to enter the law profession. As a young lawyer, he was elected to the Virginia colonial assembly, called the House of Burgesses. He was soon sent to the Continental Congress and placed on the committee to write the Declaration of Independence. His friend John Adams, also on the committee, asked him to write the first draft. The most important statement of the Declaration was that the colonies were separate from Britain, declared independent states. Jefferson also included the belief that "all men are created equal" with certain rights that cannot be taken away. That belief has helped guide Americans in self-government ever since.

After the Revolutionary War, Jefferson served in other government offices. He wrote a statute, or law, of religious freedom for Virginia, which set a standard for all the other states. Then he served as President Washington's secretary of state, in charge of foreign affairs. As an adviser to the president, Jefferson favored little government and a nation made up mostly of farmers. His point of view became the basis of one of the first American political parties, the Democratic Republican Party (an earlier form of today's Democratic Party).

Later, Jefferson became vice president to John Adams and then was elected president himself. His greatest act as president was to buy the huge Louisiana Territory from France.

After serving as president, Jefferson was happy to go home to his Virginia home, called Monticello, which he designed himself. He also founded the University of Virginia and designed its buildings.

Across

1. State where Jefferson founded a university
5. Jefferson believed these could not be taken away from people.
9. What the colonies became after the Declaration of Independence
10. Buying this territory was Jefferson's greatest accomplishment as president.
11. Jefferson was elected to this office after serving as vice president.
12. As secretary of state, Jefferson was in charge of _____ affairs.
13. Name of Jefferson's Virginia home
15. Jefferson's first government job was in the Virginia House of _____.
16. Jefferson wrote the first _____ of the Declaration of Independence.

Jefferson's Rough Draft for the Declaration of Independence

Down

1. Jefferson served under Adams as _____ president.
2. Initials of the president for whom Jefferson was secretary of state
3. Jefferson's designs for Monticello show he was skilled in this area.
4. Jefferson thought the country was best off with _____ government.
6. At the end of the Declaration of Independence, Jefferson says the colonies are now "free and _____ states."
7. Jefferson wrote an important law to guarantee this kind of freedom.
8. Initials of the man who asked Jefferson to write the first draft of the Declaration of Independence
12. Jefferson thought most Americans should work as _____.
14. Jefferson wrote that "all men are created _____."

Word List

architecture	equal	independent	Monticello	states
Burgesses	farmers	JA	president	vice
draft	foreign	little	religious	Virginia
	GW	Louisiana	rights	

GEORGE WASHINGTON

George Washington was born on a Virginia farm. He was given a primary education, then, as a young man, worked as a surveyor measuring land. When his half-brother died, Washington inherited his land and a home, Mount Vernon. Tall and strong, he liked outdoor work and the army. He became an officer in the Virginia militia and fought to push the French out of the upper Ohio River valley. In fighting at Fort Duquesne (now Pittsburgh, Pennsylvania), Washington learned Indian techniques and battle strategies.

By the end of the French and Indian War, Washington was a well-known officer. The Continental Congress asked him to become commander in chief of the Continental army in the Revolutionary War. Outnumbered by the enemy, the army never had enough supplies and were not as well trained as the British. Washington trained the army, gave them discipline, and kept up their hopes. Even in the winter of 1777–1778, when he and his men were nearly starving and freezing at Valley Forge, Washington refused to give up. His wife, Martha, joined him there and helped nurse sick soldiers. Training continued through the winter. In June 1778, the army followed Washington to a victory over the British in Monmouth, New Jersey. It was such determination, along with luck and good allies, that allowed Washington and his army to win the war.

After the Revolution, Washington tried to retire to Mount Vernon. But he was called back to become chairman of the Constitutional Convention, the gathering of delegates responsible for creating a fresh plan of government for the United States. When this plan, the Constitution, was approved, he was elected the first president of the United States and served two terms. As president, Washington helped unite the new country. He listened to arguments from all sides, then steered a middle course. He was so well known for his strength and fairness that foreign countries were willing to accept and trade with the new nation. There is little wonder that Congress decided to name the new capital city in the District of Columbia after him.

Across

1. Washington was asked to take this position at the Constitutional Convention.
3. Name of George Washington's wife
5. Colonial army; Washington joined it as a young man
8. Settlers of a new _____ on the Pacific named it after Washington.
11. Name of the fort where Washington fought during the French and Indian War
12. Mount _____ was Washington's home.
13. At Valley Forge, Washington and his men nearly starved and were almost _____.

16. Washington was the first to hold this elected position.
17. Before the Revolution, Washington was a well-known _____.

Down

George Washington

Towns, schools, and buildings have been named after the first president, including the state of Washington.

1. Washington's position in the Continental army
2. As president, Washington helped _____ the new country.
4. The city of Washington is in the _____ of Columbia.
6. What Washington inherited, with Mount Vernon on it
7. George Washington's first job
9. Number of terms Washington served as president
10. Washington learned this kind of fighting in the French and Indian War.
14. What Washington hoped to do after the Revolution
15. Martha Washington worked at this job at Valley Forge.

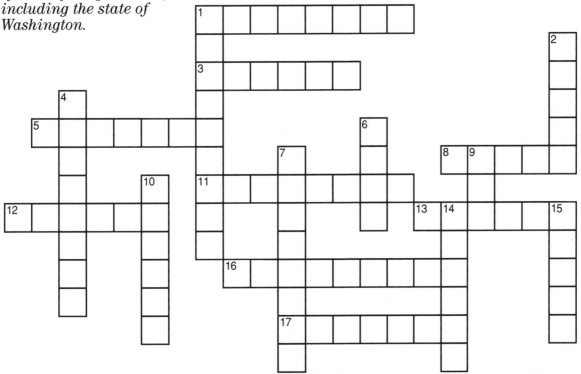

Word List

chairman	Duquesne	Martha	president	two
commander	frozen	militia	retire	unite
District	Indian	nurse	state	Vernon
	land	officer	surveyor	

23

THE CONSTITUTION

Soon after the Revolutionary War, the states began to argue with each other over trade, taxes, boundaries, and more. The Continental Congress had created a plan of government for the United States called the Articles of Confederation. But this plan made the national government so weak that it could not resolve the states' disputes. Congress decided to have a special meeting called the Constitutional Convention. The convention was held in Philadelphia in the summer of 1787 and lasted four months. There, delegates from the states created a new plan of national government: the Constitution. Delegate James Madison of Virginia kept careful notes at the Convention and offered many good ideas. For that reason, he is sometimes called the Father of the Constitution.

The Constitution created a federal system, in which states share power with a strong national government. The national government is divided into three branches (see illustration). The powers of each branch are set up with checks and balances so no single part of government becomes too powerful.

The delegates did not easily agree on this system or on other parts of the Constitution. Benjamin Franklin of Pennsylvania told the delegates they would have to compromise, just as a carpenter joins two boards by taking a little off each one. One of the most important compromises of the meeting was an agreement the small states made with the large states. All states were to have equal representation in the Senate. But the number of representatives in the House of Representatives would depend on the population of each state. This arrangement was called the Great Compromise.

Before the Constitution was approved by the states, ten amendments were added, called the Bill of Rights. The Bill of Rights gives us rights that include free speech, freedom of the press, a fair trial, and freedom of religion.

Across

2. Meeting that created the Constitution: the Constitutional _____
6. Kind of system in which states and a national government share power
7. Agreement in which each side gives up a little
10. Parts of the Constitution added after it was written
11. The Bill of Rights guarantees a ____ trial.
12. Number of branches of government
14. Name of the branch of government that makes laws
16. In this part of Congress, states are represented equally.
17. The Father of the Constitution

Government Under the Constitution

Legislative branch makes the laws (Senate, House of Representatives)

Executive branch carries out the laws (president, departments, and agencies)

Judicial branch decides what is lawful (Supreme Court, other courts)

Down

1. First ten amendments to the Constitution; the _____ of Rights
2. The government did not work well under the Articles of _____.
3. Branch of government headed by the president
4. Branch of government that decides what is lawful
5. Initials of the delegate who explained what a compromise is
8. The _____ Court heads the judicial branch.
9. Number of amendments in the Bill of Rights

13. The Constitution uses _____ and balances to keep any one part of government from becoming too powerful.
15. Name of the compromise that resulted in dividing the legislative branch into the Senate and House of Representatives

Word List

amendments	checks	executive	judicial	Supreme
BF	compromise	fair	legislative	ten
Bill	Confederation	federal	Madison	three
	Convention	Great	Senate	

LEWIS AND CLARK

In 1803, Thomas Jefferson made a deal to buy the Louisiana Territory from the French for $15 million. The land of the United States would be more than doubled. Some senators feared that this New West would overpower their eastern states, but the Senate finally approved the purchase.

Jefferson hired Meriwether Lewis and William Clark, seasoned army officers, to explore part of the purchase. Their mission was to try to find a way across the territory to the Pacific Ocean. The leaders, along with nearly fifty soldiers and assistants, headed up the Missouri River from St. Louis. They spent their first winter on the Great Plains, with the Mandan Indians. They made notes on all they saw, collected sample plants and animals, and created maps. They also hired a French Canadian guide, Toussaint Charbonneau (too-SAN shar-bohn-OH). His wife, Sacajawea (sah-kuh-juh-WEE-uh), a Shoshone (shuh-SHOH-nee), also worked as a guide and interpreter.

That spring, Lewis and Clark and their group got stuck at the foot of the Rocky Mountains. They needed horses and a good route to follow. By chance, a small group of Shoshone appeared. Sacajawea recognized her brother, now a chief. Sacajawea and her brother helped the expedition cross the mountains. When at last they reached the Pacific, Clark wrote in his journal, "Great joy!"

Lewis and Clark returned to St. Louis two years after they started, loaded with valuable information about the land they had crossed.

Across

1. Lewis's first name
4. The Shoshone woman who helped Lewis and Clark
7. Lewis and Clark brought back samples of plants and _____.
9. Indian leader; Sacajawea's brother was one
12. Relation of Sacajawea who served as guide across the Rockies
13. River that formed the eastern boundary of the Louisiana Territory
15. Tribe with whom Lewis and Clark spent their first winter
16. Lewis and Clark wintered on the Great _____.
17. Cost of Louisiana Territory, in millions of dollars

Down

1. Lewis and Clark traveled on this river upon leaving St. Louis.

The Lewis and Clark Expedition

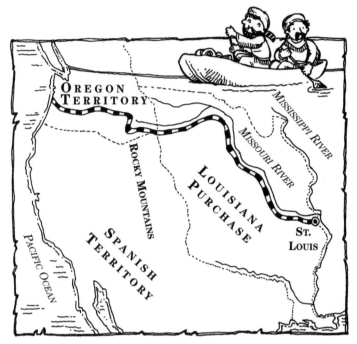

2. Mountains Lewis and Clark had to cross
3. Jefferson asked Lewis and Clark to seek a route to this ocean.
5. On seeing the Pacific, Clark wrote, "Great ___!"
6. Senators from some _____ states feared the new land would over-power them.
8. Beyond the Rockies, the expedition had to cross part of the _____ Territory.
10. Lewis and Clark drew these to guide future travelers.
11. Country that sold the Louisiana Territory to the United States
14. This government body had to approve the Louisiana Purchase.

Word List

animals	eastern	Mandan	Missouri	Rocky
brother	fifteen	maps	Oregon	Sacajawea
chief	France	Meriwether	Pacific	Senate
	joy	Mississippi	Plains	

THE OREGON TRAIL

*N*ature *at its most beautiful! Rich land for farming! Plenty of wood, water, and game!* Claims like these drew many people to the Oregon Territory in the 1840s. This area included today's Washington, Oregon, Idaho, and the Canadian province of British Columbia. The very first Americans in the Oregon Territory came to trap beaver. Some of them helped to blaze the trail route from Independence, Missouri, across the plains, over the Rocky Mountains, and to the Pacific. Called the Oregon Trail, this path made it possible for settlers to reach the Oregon Territory by wagon.

In the spring, families traveled to Independence to buy trail supplies and join a "train" of perhaps a hundred wagons. Most wagon trains included a whole herd of cattle and extra horses. Strong oxen pulled the covered wagons, called prairie "schooners," because they looked like sailing schooners on an ocean of grass.

On the open plains, wagon trains were often met by Native American bands of Kansa, Sioux, Crow, and others who traveled the land on horseback, hunting buffalo. Sometimes these people traded with the pioneers and gave directions to them.

The pioneers faced many dangers on the trail: steep mountain slopes, rushing rivers that had to be forded or crossed by raft, bad weather, and illnesses such as cholera.

Life on the Oregon Trail could also be enjoyable: People walked and talked alongside the wagons, played music around the fire, and swam in cool streams. When pioneers saw the streams flowing west instead of east, it meant they had crossed the Continental Divide and were on the last leg of their journey.

Across

1. Season in which people started on the Oregon Trail
5. Town in Missouri where the Oregon Trail began
8. Most pioneers wanted to _____ for a living when they got to Oregon.
9. Term for a line of wagons
11. When rivers were too deep to ford, a wagon could be floated on a _____.
12. This state was carved out of the Oregon Territory, along with Oregon and Idaho.
14. The Oregon Trail ended at the _____ Ocean.
15. Past the Rocky Mountains, the trail followed the _____ River.
16. West-flowing rivers showed pioneers they had crossed the _____ Divide.

Down

1. Travelers on the Oregon Trail bought most of these in Independence.
2. Large, strong, horned animals that pulled covered wagons
3. Heavy wagons could manage gradual slopes, but _____ slopes could be dangerous.
4. Animal sought by trappers in the Oregon Territory before the Trail existed
6. Native people sometimes gave pioneers _____ to help them on their way.

The Oregon Trail

7. The Oregon Trail followed this river westward when it left Missouri.
10. The animal most hunted by Plains Indians
12. Oxen pulled wagons so slowly that people could _____ beside them.
13. Initials of the Canadian province that once formed part of the Oregon Territory

Word List

BC	Continental	oxen	Snake	train
beaver	directions	Pacific	spring	walk
buffalo	farm	Platte	steep	Washington
	Independence	raft	supplies	

TEXAS

"G.T.T." was written on many house and barn doors in the South during the 1820s. It meant "Gone to Texas." Even though Texas belonged to Mexico, Americans moved there for cheap land and the freedom of the frontier.

Some of the first Americans to arrive were led by Stephen Austin, an American with a dream of founding a new western community. Unlike others, Austin had permission from Mexico to create a settlement. To get approval from Mexico, settlers were supposed to learn Spanish, become Catholic, and bring no slaves.

Soon, there were more Americans than Mexicans in Texas. Many of the Americans did not want to follow Mexican laws about religion and slavery. A new Mexican president named Antonio López de Santa Anna decided to stop the flow of Americans into Texas. He sent soldiers to take a cannon away from American Texans in the town of Gonzales, but a group of Americans fired on the soldiers. War began. In San Antonio, a small group of Americans held out for almost two weeks against the Mexican army at an old mission called the Alamo. In the end, however, Mexican soldiers killed every one of them, including two famous frontiersmen, Davy Crockett and Jim Bowie.

During the Alamo battle, other settlers were meeting in the town of San Felipe to declare Texas independent and to ask Sam Houston to lead their new army. Houston was a Texas newcomer who had been a congressman and governor of Tennessee. Houston and the army of settlers—crying "Remember the Alamo!"— quickly defeated Santa Anna. Texas remained an independent nation for nine years. Then, in 1845, it was made part of the United States. This action and others angered Mexico and led to war between the U.S. and Mexico the following year. When the United States won, it gained California and a huge territory between California and Texas.

Across

2. Texas mission, defended to the death by Americans
4. State on the Pacific coast, once part of Mexico
6. First name of a frontiersman killed at the Alamo
8. People came to Texas looking for _____ land.
9. Last name of the leader of the army that gained Texas's independence
11. Texas is one of fifty of these today.
12. Texas once belonged to _____.
13. Texas battle cry: "_____ the Alamo!"
14. Defeated Mexican leader: Santa ____

Down

1. The U.S. gained a lot of land when it won a ___ against Mexico.
2. Last name of man who started an American settlement with Mexico's permission
3. Mexico did not want this practice brought to Texas.
4. Last name of a famous frontiersman who died at the Alamo
5. The Alamo was located in the city of San _____.

Texas's First Flag

7. American settlers fought to make Texas _____.
10. Number of years Texas remained independent
11. Symbol on the first Texas flag: the "lone ____"
12. There were ____ Americans than Mexicans living in Texas when the war for independence began.

Word List

Alamo	Austin	Houston	more	star
Anna	California	independent	nine	state
Antonio	cheap	Jim	Remember	war
	Crockett	Mexico	slavery	

31

THE CALIFORNIA GOLD RUSH

"GOLD!" The headline was enough to draw more than 70,000 gold seekers to California in 1849. These "forty-niners" came from all over the world. Some followed the California Trail from the east across the Nevada desert. Others came by boat around Cape Horn at the foot of South America. The demand for fast sailing ships, called clipper ships, was so great that it helped America's ship-building industry grow.

The first gold was found by James Marshall, a millworker, in the stream water used to run a sawmill near Sacramento. The mill owner, John Sutter, had little time to celebrate before a stampede of prospectors ruined his land and business. The forty-niners hunted gold all through the foothills of the Sierra Nevada, creating mining camps and towns overnight. One result of the gold rush was the near destruction of the local Pomo Indian tribe. The Pomo were driven off the land, and many died of diseases brought in by the miners.

Few forty-niners made a fortune, but the merchants who sold goods to miners at high prices did well. San Francisco, the port where many people entered California, mushroomed into a sizable city. Gambling, stealing (or "jumping") someone's land claim, cheating, and other crimes and violence became common in the territory. There were not enough laws, courts, or police to handle these problems, which is one reason Californians voted to become a state in 1850. Sacramento, gateway to the gold region, became the state capital.

Across

3. Capital of California
7. Gold seekers would pan for gold in a river or _____.
8. Gold was found in the foothills of the Sierra _____.
9. Container used to separate gold from mud in water
10. Prospectors coming over land from the east generally used the California _____.
11. A fast sailing ship popular with forty-niners
12. Last name of the person who first found gold in California
15. Activity that increased because few laws or police existed in the gold rush days in California
16. Native American tribe badly harmed by the gold rush

Down

Gold sinks to the bottom of pan as forty-niner drains out stream water

1. Building at which gold was first discovered
2. Many gold seekers came by ship around the cape of this name.
3. Last name of the owner of the land where gold was first found
4. Gold seekers were called forty-_____.
5. This port city mushroomed during the gold rush: San _____.
6. Gold will ____ to the bottom of a pan of water.
9. These were kept very high by merchants during the gold rush.

13. California became a _____ in 1850.
14. People on the California Trail had to cross this dry area.

Word List

clipper	Francisco	niners	Sacramento	stream
crime	Horn	pan	sawmill	Sutter
desert	Marshall	Pomo	sink	Trail
	Nevada	prices	state	

SLAVERY

Slavery might have died out sooner in the United States were it not for Eli Whitney's invention of the cotton gin in 1793. This machine cleaned the seeds out of cotton so well that it made growing cotton a more profitable business. While northern states largely gave up slavery and built mills and factories, southern states became a land of cotton and other crops grown on large farms called plantations. So much cotton grew in the South that people there called it King Cotton.

One in four southern families kept slaves, most holding only a few as farmhands or servants. But the big plantation owners kept many. Most slaves there worked as field hands in gangs of thirty to forty men, women, and children. They were directed by a white overseer or by another slave called the driver. Other slaves worked in their owner's household or at crafts like woodworking. Slaves had little free time and were not allowed education except for some churchgoing. However, slaves developed their own arts and traditions, based partly on the African ways of their ancestors. Music sung and played by slaves became the basis of jazz, the blues, and much of modern American popular music.

Some slaves tried to revolt. Nat Turner led a slave revolt in which some white families were killed. It resulted in harsher laws to control slaves. Others escaped to northern states or non-slavery countries. A network of black and white people who helped slaves escape was called the Underground Railroad. Former slave Harriet Tubman helped lead more than 300 people to freedom through that system. Even though no actual railroad existed, such helpers were called conductors, and houses where escaping slaves could rest in hiding were called stations.

Across

1. The cotton gin made growing cotton more _____.
4. Slaves learned something in this institution.
6. Last name of the inventor of the cotton gin
8. _____ Turner led a slave rebellion.
10. The _____ Railroad helped slaves escape.
14. Continent that was a source for slave arts and traditions
16. Most of the world's supply of this crop grew in the South.
17. Group of field hands that worked together
18. Term for people who helped slaves escape on the Underground Railroad

Down

Some Routes of the Underground Railroad

2. One of every _____ families in the South owned slaves.
3. Country south of Texas to which some slaves escaped
5. Country north of the United States to which some slaves escaped
7. Plantation slaves worked in the fields, as craftsmen, or in the owner's _____.
9. Last name of a famous African American conductor on the Underground Railroad
11. Slave drivers were usually _____ themselves.
12. Because so much was grown, cotton was called this in the South.
13. The _____ created by slaves became the basis of jazz and the blues.
15. In this area, states ended slavery and built more factories.

Word List

Africa	conductors	household	Nat	Tubman
Canada	cotton	King	North	Underground
church	four	Mexico	profitable	Whitney
	gang	music	slaves	

FREDERICK DOUGLASS

Frederick Douglass was a great African American speaker. He was a leader in the abolition movement to end slavery in the United States. Douglass was born a slave with the name Frederick Bailey on a plantation in Maryland. As a boy he was sent to serve in a city house in Baltimore. There, his master's wife began to teach him to read and write—until her husband stopped her. Douglass kept learning on his own. He blacked, or polished, boots to earn money, then paid a white boy to get his first book. Soon he was writing out passes, allowing runaway slaves to claim they were free.

As a young man, Douglass was sent to learn ship caulking. He managed to escape his place of work, taking a train to New York. For safety, he changed his name from Bailey to Douglass and moved farther north into Massachusetts. There he worked as a day laborer. One day, he spoke up at an abolition meeting. He spoke so well that he was hired by the Massachusetts Anti-Slavery Society to lecture in other towns. Douglass told about the evils of slavery, especially the breaking up of slave family members. He had in mind the master who had split him from his own mother at birth, then separated him from a loving grandmother when he was a child.

Douglass wrote a book telling the story of his life and started his own paper, the *North Star*. He believed African Americans should lead in the struggle for their own freedom. He used his house in Rochester, New York, as a station in the Underground Railroad to hide escaping slaves.

When the Civil War began, Douglass was one of the first to urge that African Americans be allowed to serve in the Union army. He was too old to fight himself, but his two sons joined the army. In old age, he lived an honored life in Washington, D.C., where he held various offices, including U.S. minister to Haiti.

Across

5. Douglass was most famous as a _____ for the abolition of slavery.
6. City where Douglass lived in old age
9. When the master found out, his wife had to ____ teaching Douglass.
12. City where Douglass grew up and learned to read
13. Relatives of Douglass who fought in the Civil War
14. State where Douglass was born on a plantation
15. Douglass especially hated the _____ of slave family members.
17. Two-letter abbreviation of the state where Douglass began his speaking career
18. Two-letter abbreviation of the state to which Douglass went to escape slavery

Down

Frederick Douglass

1. Douglass's job when he first escaped slavery
2. Country where Douglass served as U.S. minister
3. Douglass's last name when he was a slave
4. In Rochester, Douglass used his home as an Underground Railroad _____.
7. Term used for the idea of ending slavery
8. Douglass wrote one of these about his own life.
10. Young Douglass wrote free _____ for runaway slaves.
11. Douglass blacked these to earn money for a book.
16. Douglass urged that African Americans be allowed to join this.

Word List

abolition	Baltimore	laborer	passes	station
army	book	MA	separation	stop
Bailey	boots	Maryland	sons	Washington
	Haiti	NY	speaker	

ABRAHAM LINCOLN

Abraham Lincoln was born in 1809 in a Kentucky log cabin, then moved with his family to farms on the frontier in Indiana and in Illinois. He educated himself by reading, and in 1834, he became a legislator, helping make laws for the state of Illinois. In 1836, he became a lawyer. Lincoln married a Kentucky woman, Mary Todd, and in time they had four sons. Lincoln became nationally famous when he ran for U.S. Senate against Stephen Douglas. In a series of public arguments called the Lincoln-Douglas Debates, Lincoln declared the nation could not last "half slave and half free."

The Republican Party made Lincoln their candidate for president in 1860. He won, and only a month after his election, the rebel Confederate states were at war with the United States. On January 1, 1863, he freed the slaves in the rebelling states with the Emancipation Proclamation. His aim was to discourage the South with the proclamation. Lincoln always said he was personally against slavery, but he thought the union of the states was the most important issue. Midway through the war, Lincoln spoke at a battlefield near Gettysburg, Pennsylvania. He asked Americans to stick to the ideals of freedom and equality for which many men had died.

When he was reelected as president toward the end of the war, Lincoln promised that the government would act "with malice [meanness] toward none, with charity [kindness, generosity] for all." However, Lincoln was shot while he sat in a theater shortly after the end of the war by John Wilkes Booth, a man still angry about the South's loss. The assassin's bullet did not stop the ideals Lincoln worked for: freedom, equality, and national unity.

Across

3. Lincoln's statue in Washington, D.C., is called the Lincoln _____.
6. Lincoln sought to heal the nation "with _____ toward none."
8. Lincoln's political party
10. State where Lincoln was born
12. State where Lincoln first was elected to public office
13. Lincoln was president during the Civil ___.
15. Number of sons Lincoln had
16. Last name of person who debated with Lincoln in a Senate campaign
17. Lincoln's nickname

Down

The Lincoln Memorial in Washington, D.C.

1. Term for freeing slaves; used in name of Lincoln's famous proclamation
2. Kind of building in which Lincoln was born
4. First name of Lincoln's wife
5. Lincoln was one of the greatest in this office.
7. Rebelling states called themselves _____ states.
9. Last name of the assassin who shot Lincoln
11. National _____ was one of Lincoln's greatest goals.
14. Lincoln did this to educate himself.
15. Lincoln said no nation could long exist "half slave and half ____."

Word List

Abe	Confederate	free	Mary	Republican
Booth	Douglas	Illinois	Memorial	unity
cabin	emancipation	Kentucky	president	War
	four	malice	read	

FIGHTING THE CIVIL WAR

When Abraham Lincoln was elected president in 1860, South Carolina decided to leave, or secede from, the Union. However, Fort Sumter, on the Carolina coast, remained in the hands of the U.S. Army. Angry state officials had the fort bombarded, and the Civil War began.

Eleven states in the South united to form the Confederacy, headed by Jefferson Davis. Robert E. Lee, once a U.S. Army officer, agreed to lead the Confederate army. Lincoln named several generals to lead the Union army, but finally he came to depend most on Ulysses S. Grant.

Lincoln decided to weaken the South by cutting off its oceangoing trade with a naval blockade. Meanwhile, the North, with lots more factories and people, was well supplied.

Many soldiers were killed in the war, partly because improved rifles and cannons killed more efficiently than the older models. Even more men died, however, because of infected wounds and diseases that swept the camps and military prisons.

Midway through the war, Lincoln freed slaves in the rebelling states with the Emancipation Proclamation. Since slaves in the rebelling states were under the power of the Confederacy, the Proclamation did not set slaves free immediately. However, it paved the way for a complete end to slavery after the war.

Although the South won major battles early in the war, the tide turned at Gettysburg, Pennsylvania. There, the Union turned back General Lee's attempt to invade the northern states. In battles at Vicksburg and Chattanooga, the Union gained control of western Confederate states. Then, while Grant pushed southward, Union General William Sherman's men made a long march through Georgia to the sea. His troops burned crops and houses, destroying anything that could help the Confederate army stay alive. Finally, Lee surrendered to Grant at the Appomattox Courthouse in Virginia, on April 9, 1865.

Across

1. The first full battle of the Civil War was at _____ Run, near Washington, D.C.
4. The North had more of these to make arms and supplies.
7. Location of an important battle in Mississippi
9. Initials of the most important Union general
11. Number of states in the Confederacy
12. Lee did this at Appomattox Courthouse.
13. The Civil War was mostly fought in this area, rather than in the North.
14. Last name of the Union general who destroyed property across the South
15. Last name of the leader of the Confederacy

Down

Important Civil War Battles and Who Won Them

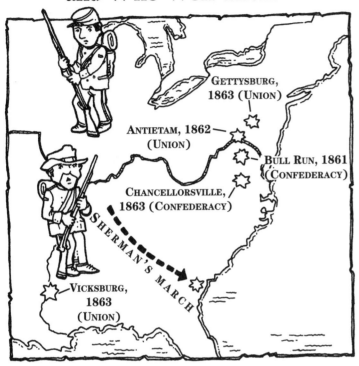

1. Line of ships used to stop trade with the South
2. Last name of the general who led the Confederate army
3. State where the Confederates surrendered
5. The Emancipation Proclamation ended this in the Confederacy.
6. Cause of more soldiers' deaths than gunfire
8. Lincoln had several of these but depended most on Grant.
9. The side that won the battle at Gettysburg
10. Name of the fort where the Civil War started
14. Initials of the state that was first to secede

Word List

blockade	disease	Lee	South	USG
Bull	eleven	SC	Sumter	Vicksburg
Davis	factories	Sherman	surrender	Virginia
	generals	slavery	Union	

RECONSTRUCTION

Reconstruction means "rebuilding." After the Civil War, the president and Congress struggled over the best way to rebuild the South. President Andrew Johnson put in place a plan of reconstruction that allowed states of the old Confederacy to rejoin the Union easily. Soon most Southern states had passed laws called the black codes, which kept freedmen (former slaves) from voting, assembling, or working at many jobs. Congress did establish a Freedmen's Bureau to help the former slaves. The bureau founded over 4,000 schools in five years. Adults often attended these schools along with the children to learn how to read and write.

Congress grew angry over the way the new state governments were treating the freedmen. It passed amendments to the Constitution to guarantee citizens' rights. When some states refused to accept the amendments, Congress sent the army back to the South to enforce them. Congress also passed Reconstruction Acts in 1867 that required real changes. Under the acts, new representatives were elected in the South, including the first African Americans in government. The new state governments raised taxes to pay for rebuilding, though some of the money went into the pockets of selfish politicians. Northerners came south to help with the reconstruction—or to make a profit. White Southerners named them all after the cheap suitcase of the day: carpetbaggers.

By 1877, Reconstruction had died out in the South. Why? White Southerners in general resented Reconstruction bitterly. Some people were making unfair profits from it. And Congress lost interest. Then, violence by secret groups like the Ku Klux Klan kept African Americans from voting or getting good jobs. Many black people lived in poverty as sharecroppers, working the land for a share of the crop. Most of them were always paying off debts—money borrowed so they could live until harvest time.

Across

3. Name for rebuilding after the Civil War
6. Southern term for a Northerner in the South during Reconstruction
8. The Fifteenth Amendment guarantees the right of a citizen to ____.
9. The black _____ were laws keeping freed slaves from full rights.
10. The Fourteenth Amendment gives equal _____ of the laws to all citizens.
11. The Fourteenth Amendment says all people ____ in the U.S. are citizens.
15. Someone who farms for a part of the crop
16. Under Johnson's plan, it was easy for one of these to reenter the Union.
17. Number of the constitutional amendment that ended slavery

Down

1. First part of the name of a secret violent white group in the South
2. Last name of the U.S. president during Reconstruction

13. SLAVERY IS ILLEGAL.

14. EVERYONE BORN IN THE UNITED STATES IS A CITIZEN. ALL CITIZENS HAVE EQUAL PROTECTION UNDER THE LAW.

15. ALL CITIZENS HAVE THE RIGHT TO VOTE, WHATEVER THEIR RACE, COLOR, OR PREVIOUS CONDITION UNDER SLAVERY.

Three great amendments to the Constitution that were passed after the Civil War

4. The president struggled with this group over Reconstruction.
5. The Freedmen's Bureau established over 4,000 of these.
7. The Freedmen's _____ helped the recently freed slaves.
8. Used by secret white groups in the South to keep freedmen from power or success
12. Organization used by Congress to enforce Reconstruction
13. Money collected by government for Reconstruction
14. Sharecroppers' profits often went to pay these.

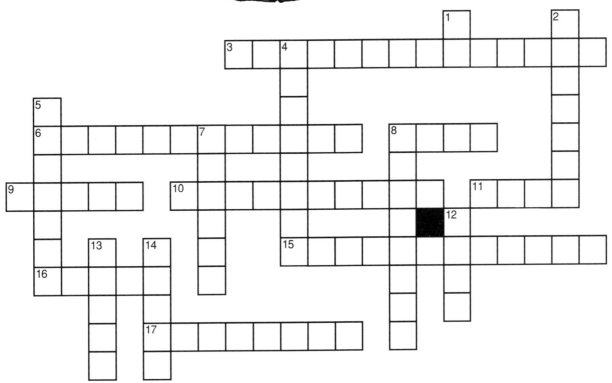

Word List

army	carpetbagger	Johnson	schools	thirteen
born	codes	Ku	sharecropper	violence
Bureau	Congress	protection	state	vote
	debts	Reconstruction	taxes	

WOMEN'S RIGHTS

All men and women are created equal." This statement was at the heart of a declaration made at the first women's rights convention, held at Seneca Falls, New York, in 1848. The organizers of the conference, Lucretia Mott and Elizabeth Cady Stanton, were active in the abolition movement. As they argued that slaves should have freedom and rights, they realized that women should, too.

American women were not allowed to vote. In many states, women were not even allowed to own property or keep their own wages. Most jobs and colleges were closed to them.

Many women took part in the struggle to change all this. The Grimké sisters, Sarah and Angelina, asked lawmakers to consider freedom for women as well as freedom for slaves. Sojourner Truth, herself a former slave, pointed out that women could work as hard as men.

One of the greatest workers for women's rights was Susan B. Anthony. She lectured and organized tirelessly all her life. Anthony met Elizabeth Cady Stanton soon after the Seneca Falls conference. Stanton became Anthony's speechwriter and good friend. They led the struggle for a New York law allowing women to keep their own wages. It became a model for laws in other states.

The fight for woman suffrage, or the right of women to vote, lasted many decades. Anthony and other early leaders did not live to see their ideal gained. At last in 1920, the Nineteenth Amendment was passed, allowing all women in the United States the right to vote.

Across

3. Term for the right to vote
6. Many women first fought for the freedom and rights of these people.
8. The New York law allowing women to keep their wages served as a _____ for other states to follow.
9. Susan B. _____, great women's rights leader
11. One of the first states to give women the right to some voting
13. Kind of meeting held in Seneca Falls for women's rights
14. First college to admit both men and women
15. Land or houses; women were not allowed to own this in many states
16. Stanton was a _____ of speeches for Anthony.

Important Places for Women's Rights

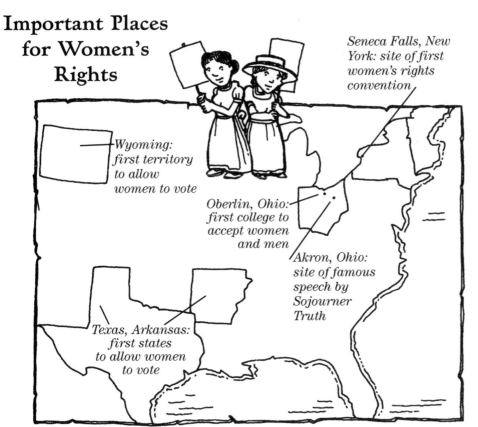

Seneca Falls, New York: site of first women's rights convention

Wyoming: first territory to allow women to vote

Oberlin, Ohio: first college to accept women and men

Akron, Ohio: site of famous speech by Sojourner Truth

Texas, Arkansas: first states to allow women to vote

Down

1. Location of first women's rights convention: _____ Falls
2. Large state that allowed women to vote early
3. _____ Truth, former slave who spoke for women's rights
4. Movement that awakened some women to their lack of rights
5. When full suffrage was gained, early leaders of the movement were already ____.
6. Last name of Anthony's friend and fellow worker for women's rights

7. Two-letter abbreviation of the state that, as a territory, first gave women the vote
10. Women once were not allowed to keep property or their own _____.
12. Last name of sisters who worked for abolition and women's rights

Word List

abolition	convention	Oberlin	Sojourner	wages
Anthony	dead	property	Stanton	writer
Arkansas	Grimké	Seneca	suffrage	WY
	model	slaves	Texas	

THE FATE OF THE INDIANS

From the first arrival of Europeans on the East Coast, Indians were pushed westward. In 1830, Congress tried to end problems between settlers and Indians. The Indian Removal Act forced all Indians living east of the Mississippi River to move far west to the land that is now Oklahoma. Earlier agreements and treaties were broken as many tribes were forced to leave their homelands. The Cherokee Indians lost about a quarter of their people on the trail to disease, cold, and hunger. For that reason, the journey to Oklahoma was called the Trail of Tears.

After the Civil War, the buffalo-hunting tribes of the Great Plains lost more and more game and land to settlers. The government tried to keep the Indians on plots of land set aside for them, called reservations. There, they were supposed to farm instead of hunt. But the Sioux and other tribes wanted freedom to move and hunt as they had done before. The U.S. Army came to the plains to protect settlers and enforce the reservation law. Full battles between the army and various tribes sometimes resulted. In 1876, in what is now Montana, Sioux warriors wiped out General George Custer and all of his men at the Battle of the Little Bighorn (also called Custer's Last Stand). Within a year, though, the Sioux leader, Crazy Horse, had to surrender to the army. Nez Percé people, from Oregon, fled across Idaho and Montana to try to escape into Canada. The army caught them and their leader, Chief Joseph, just before they reached the border. Chief Joseph spoke for many Indians when he said, "My heart is sick and sad." The Nez Percé were sent to a reservation.

In 1887, Congress passed the Dawes Act. The act said only individual Indians, not tribes, had the right to hold land. Millions of acres of reservation land were sold off to non-Indians. It was not until the 1930s that this policy ended. Then, a new law stopped the breakup of tribal lands, allowed native peoples to govern themselves on reservations, and encouraged tribes to keep their traditions and customs.

Across

2. Plains tribe, most living north of the Canadian border
9. Tribe living in the farthest southwest part of the plains
10. State on land where eastern tribes were forced to move
11. Chief of the Nez Percé
12. Areas set aside for tribes by the government
14. The Dawes Act brought an ___ to tribal land ownership.
15. The army caught the Nez Percé before they could enter _____.
16. Tribe that (with some Cheyenne) defeated Custer
17. Tribe that lost a quarter of its people on the way to Oklahoma

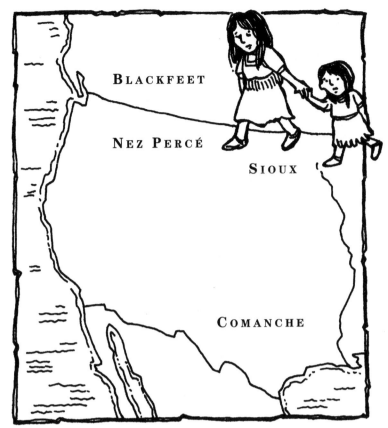

As America expanded, Native American tribes were forced to move farther west.

Down

1. The Nez _____ originally lived on the northeast edge of the plains.
2. Custer was defeated at the Battle of the Little _____.
3. Plains Indians needed ample land on which to ____ buffalo.
4. Under the Dawes Act, much reservation land was ____.
5. The Trail of Tears resulted from the Indian _____ Act.
6. Custer's position in the U.S. Army
7. Second word in the name of the Sioux chief who defeated Custer
8. Name of the act that allowed only individual Indians to own land
13. These groups could no longer own land under the Dawes Act.

Word List

Bighorn	Cherokee	general	Oklahoma	Sioux
Blackfeet	Comanche	Horse	Percé	sold
Canada	Dawes	hunt	Removal	tribes
	end	Joseph	reservations	

HOMESTEADING

During the Civil War, Congress passed the Homestead Act. It gave citizens or immigrants 160 acres of land on the Great Plains if they settled there for five years. The aim was to create many small farms from Wisconsin westward. At the same time, new railroads tried to encourage settlement in order to get more business. They sold land they had bought or that had been granted to them by the government when their lines were built.

People came from the eastern United States and from many other countries to homestead. They found treeless prairie covered with tough-rooted grass. A steel plow could cut through the roots, but often there was not enough water. Homesteaders learned "dry farming," in which grains are planted deep to catch moisture low in the soil.

Homesteaders learned other ways to get along on the plains. Without enough wood, they built houses called soddies from blocks of root-filled earth. Their fires burned with dry buffalo droppings called chips. To pump up drinking water, they built windmills to catch the prairie wind. They learned the importance of planting trees to hold the soil once the prairie grass was plowed.

The new farmers faced many problems: blizzards, fires, drought, and sometimes grasshoppers that ate everything from crops to boots! Even at home in their sod houses, people were irritated by snakes and insects falling from the ceiling. Yet homesteading still drew people. In 1893, a last bit of land was opened for homesteading: the Cherokee Outlet in Oklahoma. Over 100,000 people lined the Kansas border to rush in when the signal was given.

Across

3. Transportation business that sold plains land
4. Winter storms that ruined homesteaders' land
6. People used windmills to ____ water for drinking and watering gardens.
7. Machine that used the wind as an energy source
10. Insect that ate homesteaders' crops
13. Number of years a homesteader had to stay on claimed land
14. Animal that sometimes dropped from a sod roof
15. Nickname for a sod house
16. Source of wood; scarce on the plains

Down

1. Long time without water; dangerous to crops
2. The _____ Act allowed people to claim land on the plains.

4. Homesteaders burned the dry droppings of this animal.
5. Size of homestead farms; opposite of large
8. A living hazard of soddie life, besides snakes
9. Kind of farming that required little water
11. Kind of plow that would cut through prairie sod

12. People lined up along the Kansas _____ to get land in the Cherokee Outlet.
13. A hot danger that left the prairie black

Word List

blizzards	drought	grasshopper	railroad	steel
border	dry	Homestead	small	tree
buffalo	fire	insects	snake	windmill
	five	pump	soddie	

COWBOYS

The first American cowboys were really Mexicans. They raised longhorn cattle in Texas while it was still part of Mexico. Most features of cowboy life developed there. The main job of a cowboy was to move herds of steers from place to place and to protect the animals on the open land. Texas cowboys used a well-trained small horse that could turn easily to stop and steer the cattle. They threw a rope loop called a lasso to catch individual animals. They marked cows with a branding iron to show who owned them. Branding was necessary because herds often mixed on the plains, and land ownership was not clear. Texas cowboys wore leather leggings called chaps to protect their legs from brush and cactus. Cowboy hats developed from the broad Mexican sombrero.

Cowboys moved north when the first railroads came to Kansas and Missouri. Texan cattle owners realized that if they could get animals to the railroad, they could ship them to Chicago for slaughter and sale to eastern cities. People there paid well for good beef. Every spring, cowboys were hired by the cattle owners to drive huge herds north to the railroad.

A cattle drive took many weeks, since a herd could only travel about fifteen miles a day. Cowboys kept the thousands of cows together and guarded against rustlers (thieves) and stampedes. To calm the herd, cowboys sang to them. Cowboy songs became an important part of American popular music.

As the nation expanded westward, longhorns were kept not only in Texas, but also on huge open grasslands called ranges all over the plains. In some sparsely settled areas, cattle owners took the place of government. Their decisions were called "cow custom," which meant the law of the herd owners. After barbed wire was invented in 1873, farmers fenced their land to keep out cattle. Soon the herd owners and cowboys themselves were building fences to create enclosed ranches, and the wandering cowboy life came to an end.

Across

4. Uncontrolled rush of cattle; something cowboys had to control
7. Starting point of cattle trails that went north to the railroad
10. Cattle were first shipped to this city for slaughter.
11. Cattle thief
12. City in Kansas; destination of the Chisholm Trail
13. Animal used by cowboys to help herd cows
15. Term for rope used to catch cows
16. Texas cowboys used a branding _____.
17. Owners of these eventually fenced them to keep in cattle.

Down

1. Leather leggings cowboys wore to protect against brush
2. Many items used by cowboys were originally used by those of this nationality
3. Cowboy clothing item based on the sombrero
5. About the number of miles a herd could travel in a day
6. Community decisions made by cattle owners were called cow _____ .
8. Kind of cattle raised in Texas
9. Term for taking a herd to a distant location: cattle _____
10. Name of cattle trail that started at San Antonio
14. Open grazing land

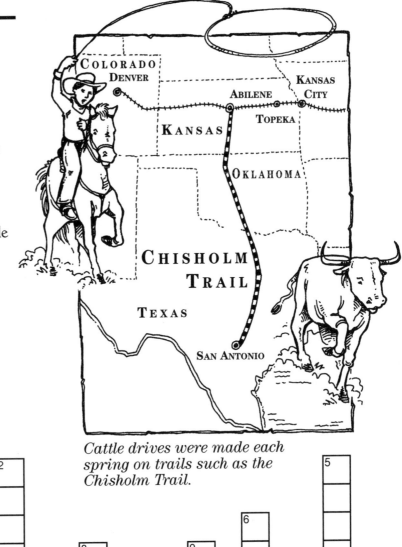

Cattle drives were made each spring on trails such as the Chisholm Trail.

Word List

Abilene	Chisholm	hat	longhorn	rustler
chaps	custom	horse	Mexican	stampede
Chicago	drive	iron	ranches	Texas
	fifteen	lasso	range	

INVENTIONS

Thomas Edison was called the Wizard of Menlo Park because he and the people working in his Menlo Park, New Jersey, laboratory produced over 1,000 inventions after the Civil War. The greatest was the electric lightbulb. Edison also invented the phonograph and one of the first motion picture cameras.

Edison was not the only inventor hard at work between the middle 1800s and into the early twentieth century. Alexander Graham Bell invented the telephone in 1876. Guglielmo Marconi (gool-YEL-moh mar-COH-nee), an Italian, invented the wireless telegraph, which led to radio. The American press gave huge coverage to Marconi's experiment in which a signal from England was received in North America. And Dr. John Kellogg invented cornflakes! His first cold cereal went along with other inventions that made food easier to keep and prepare, such as home canning and refrigeration.

These and many other inventions helped a great change to come about called the Industrial Revolution. This revolution was a change from work done by hand to work done by machines. The Industrial Revolution was first set in motion in England, where the steam engine was invented. The first American factories, built in the early 1800s in New England, spun yarn and wove cloth using power from a wheel turned by water. Beginning in the middle 1800s, steam engines powered factories, boats, and trains. In Pennsylvania, Edwin Drake first drilled for oil that was used to grease the engines and served as a valuable fuel. Trains began to roll on steel rails instead of iron because the new Bessemer process created long-lasting steel more quickly and cheaply than old-style steel. Strong steel lay at the heart of many inventions, from the typewriter to the skyscraper to the barbed wire used especially by farmers and ranchers in the west.

Across

2. Last name of the inventor of the cornflake
6. The Industrial _____ expanded in the United States after the Civil War.
9. Kind of wire used to keep animals in or out
12. Edison invented the _____bulb.
14. This invention helped people talk over long distances.
15. Process that made steel quicker and cheaper to produce
16. Edison was called this as a nickname.
17. Tall building based on a steel frame
18. Last name of first person to drill in the earth for large amounts of oil

Some Inventions of the 19th Century

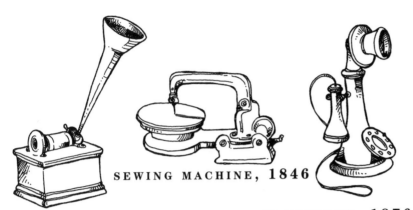

PHONOGRAPH, 1863

SEWING MACHINE, 1846

TELEPHONE, 1876

Down

1. Initials of the inventor of the telephone
3. Last name of the inventor who, with his laboratory partners, invented over 1,000 things
4. With a _____ machine, clothes could be made more quickly.
5. Substance that powered engines in the second half of the 1800s
7. Last name of the inventor of the wireless telegraph
8. Made of steel, these were laid all over the United States after the Civil War.

10. Substance that powered the first American factories
11. Strong, long-lasting material used in many inventions
13. Oil was used to _____ engines so they would run smoothly.

Word List

AGB	**Drake**	**light**	**sewing**	**telephone**
barbed	**Edison**	**Marconi**	**skyscraper**	**water**
Bessemer	**grease**	**rails**	**steam**	**wizard**
	Kellogg	**Revolution**	**steel**	

BIG BUSINESS

The late 1800s brought a huge growth spurt to American business. American stores, for instance, became larger to sell the many new products being invented and produced. Before, people had to go to several small shops to find what they wanted. Now, large department stores opened in cities, offering such items as clothes, shoes, furniture, and food, all under one roof. Woolworth's and J.C. Penney also appeared as early chain stores, which were nearly identical stores under the same ownership, sprinkled all across the country. Sears, Roebuck and Co. and other stores sold their products for the first time through catalogues sent nationwide. This was the beginning of the mail-order catalogue business, today a multibillion-dollar industry.

Larger and larger companies were creating the products people bought. John D. Rockefeller founded one of the largest: the Standard Oil Company. Standard Oil first grew by buying up other oil producers and oil refiners. Rockefeller joined these companies into a new type of business organization called a trust. In a trust, a central board of directors reduces competition among its companies and sets prices. When one organization sells nearly all of the available supply of one product, as Rockefeller did with American oil, it is called a monopoly. A monopoly can be dangerous because it can keep prices for its goods high without worrying about another business selling the same thing for less.

Many people were upset when big businesses destroyed smaller ones and forced buyers to pay high prices. The government responded to the public feeling with the Sherman Antitrust Act of 1890. The law was supposed to keep trusts from ending competition. The law turned out to be difficult to enforce, but it showed that government could have a role in setting business rules.

Business owners defended themselves against public criticism by saying they increased economic activity and so helped the nation. Andrew Carnegie, owner of a huge steel company, argued that rich businesspeople should use their money to help other people. At the end of his life, Carnegie gave his money to found public libraries all over the nation and to help build hospitals and schools.

Across

2. One set of officers controls competition and prices among several companies in this form of business.
4. Name of the government's antitrust act
5. From this book, customers could order goods by mail.
8. Building full of books; Carnegie paid for many

This cartoon from the late 19th century shows how rich business owners had the reputation for caring about nothing except money and golf.

10. Name of the oil company Rockefeller founded
11. A business controlling all of one product
14. Kind of store selling many sorts of things under one roof
15. Rockefeller bought out both oil producers and oil _____.
16. A place where early department stores were located

Down

1. Product that made Carnegie rich
3. John D. _____ created one of the first trusts.
4. Example of a mail-order catalogue store
5. He made a fortune in steel, then gave much of it away.
6. The Sherman Antitrust Act showed that _____ had a role in making rules for business.
7. The press showed concern that all rich people cared about was this.
9. A monopoly can control the _____ of goods.
12. What U.S. stores became in the late 1800s
13. Kind of store that sells the same items in many locations

Word List

Carnegie	city	library	refiners	Standard
catalogue	department	money	Rockefeller	steel
chain	government	monopoly	Sears	trust
	larger	price	Sherman	

IMMIGRATION

After the Civil War and through the early years of the twentieth century, a great wave of people came to live in the United States from other countries. Before 1880, most of these immigrants were from northwestern European countries including Ireland, Britain, Germany, and the Scandinavian nations. After 1880, more and more came from southeastern Europe, from such countries as Italy, Greece, Poland, and Russia.

Late in the 1800s, little open land remained for farming, but the rapidly growing cities offered jobs in factories. Poor immigrants lived in crowded conditions, many in poorly built apartment buildings called tenements. They worked for low wages, often in sweatshops. These were small factories where hours were long and the pay low. Most immigrants felt that education was the key to a better life. Immigrant children filled the public schools, and many adults went to school at night.

Many of the immigrants who settled on the West Coast were Asian. Chinese people first arrived in large numbers to prospect for gold in 1849, and, later, to work on the railroads. Chinese workers laid most of the track for the Central Pacific Railroad, which ran from California eastward to Utah, where it joined the Union Pacific to become the first transcontinental railroad—a railroad spanning across the continent. Many Japanese people came to the United States to work on orchards and farms. Both Japanese and Chinese immigrants faced prejudice—negative opinions about them because of their race. In 1882, Congress passed the first of a set of laws to keep Chinese people out of the country. In the 1920s, Congress decided to control all immigration through quotas—limits on the number of immigrants from a region or country. The quotas ended three centuries of unlimited immigration. The quota system based on country of origin was done away with in 1965.

Across

4. Full of people; describes the tenements of the late 1800s
5. This country gave the Statue of Liberty to the United States as a gift in 1886.
7. A kind of railroad; Chinese workers helped build the first one
11. Immigrants pinned their hopes for the future on this.
13. A crowded, cheap apartment building
14. In sweatshops, hours were ____.
16. The _____ of Liberty stands in New York harbor.
17. Congress passed the first ___ to keep Chinese people out in 1882.
18. Someone who comes to live permanently in a new country from another country

Down

1. Part of Europe from which most immigrants came before 1880
2. Small factories where people worked long hours for low pay in bad conditions
3. Negative opinion of a group of people based on race

The Statue of Liberty, a gift from France, greets immigrants in New York harbor.

6. Asian immigrants who worked largely on West Coast farms
8. The quota system was designed to _____ all immigration.
9. Places where most immigrants in the late 1800s settled to find jobs
10. Many Asian immigrants settled on the ___ Coast.
12. Immigrants from this country were banned from the United States in 1882.
15. Many Chinese immigrants first came to California to seek this.

Word List

China	crowded	immigrant	northwestern	tenement
cities	education	Japanese	prejudice	transcontinental
control	France	law	Statue	West
	gold	long	sweatshops	

JANE ADDAMS

Jane Addams helped make life better in American cities. She was born into a wealthy family in Cedarville, Illinois. As a young woman, she visited London. In a poor neighborhood there, she visited Toynbee Hall, a "settlement house" where students from Oxford University were helping people. Addams decided to try to do something similar in her home state. She used her own inherited money to start the project.

With a friend, Ellen Gates Starr, she leased a house in a run-down, rat-infested neighborhood in Chicago and called it Hull House. The two friends opened a reading room and a kindergarten. Soon, Hull House was offering cooking, health, and English classes for poor immigrants. Neighborhood people were welcome to come for help in everything from finding a place to live to learning to sew. Addams worked to get the city to improve garbage collection and sewers. Hull House also acted as a center for the arts, with an art gallery and a music school. People paid a small amount for Hull House services. The point was not to give away charity but to help people become independent. By 1895, Addams's idea had been imitated in fifty more settlement houses in American cities. Many such houses exist today.

Addams did more than run Hull House. She worked especially hard for poor children. She helped end child labor in Illinois and worked to create juvenile courts, where children accused of crimes could be treated differently from adults. Addams thought fun was important, too. She sent city children to country summer camps and helped create the first public playground in Chicago.

Across

2. Addams helped set up _____ courts for children.
4. People were expected to ___ a small amount for Hull House services.
5. Immigrants could learn this language at Hull House.
6. City where Hull House was founded
9. Hull House had an art _____.
11. Term used for a city social services institution: ____ house
13. Students from this university helped run Toynbee Hall.
14. A room for this was one of the first things Addams established at Hull House.
15. Opposite of dependent; what Addams wanted people to be

Jane Addams, a woman who was devoted to helping others, especially poor children

Down

1. What Addams used to pay for Hull House
3. Addams helped improve life in these.
4. Addams established the first of these in Chicago, just for children.
7. First word in name of Addams's settlement house
8. Number of settlement houses in the United States by 1895
9. Addams convinced the city to collect this better.
10. Rodents that are a city health hazard
11. Last name of the friend who helped Addams set up Hull House
12. First word in the name of the London house that inspired Addams

Word List

Chicago	fifty	independent	pay	settlement
cities	gallery	inheritance	playground	Starr
English	garbage	juvenile	rats	Toynbee
	Hull	Oxford	reading	

THEODORE ROOSEVELT

Theodore Roosevelt's life spanned both the nineteenth and twentieth centuries. He helped the nation move into modern times. Born in New York City in 1858, Roosevelt was, as he said himself, a "sickly" boy. He learned to box, wrestle, and hunt to become stronger. He threw himself into all he did with great energy. He attended Harvard College, then divided his time between New York politics and writing. For two years he ran a ranch in the Dakota Territory.

Roosevelt became nationally known during the Spanish-American War of 1898. The war began when Spain refused to give Cuba independence, and the United States sided with Cuba. Roosevelt collected friends, some of them western cowboys, to go and fight in Cuba. These "Rough Riders" helped win the war against Spain.

Famous as a Rough Rider, Roosevelt was elected governor of New York, then vice president of the United States. He became the youngest president in history when President McKinley was shot in 1901. Roosevelt was popular and liked to have fun. On a hunting trip, he refused to shoot a bear cub. Quickly, a toy maker created the "Teddy Bear" to remember the event. The stuffed bear became a popular American toy.

Roosevelt liked to say people should have a fair, or "square," deal. He became the first president to step between owners and workers when a coal strike created hardships. He threatened to seize the mines if owners would not agree to talk. The owners did agree, and finally the two sides settled fairly. Roosevelt had the Justice Department sue a northwestern railroad monopoly for stopping business competition. It was the first of his many moves to "bust trusts," which means to break up combinations of businesses that are controlling prices. He also worked to set up the Pure Food and Drug Act, which still protects American food safety. Finally, he loved nature; he added to the national parks and created national forests and wildlife refuges—places where animals could not be hunted.

Across

4. Roosevelt was elected governor of New _____.
6. Caribbean island other than Cuba gained by the United States in the Spanish-American War
8. Roosevelt lived the second part of his life in this century.
10. Describes Roosevelt as president; opposite of oldest
12. Combinations of companies, which Roosevelt broke up
13. Roosevelt worked to pass the ____ Food and Drug Act.
15. Word Roosevelt used to describe himself as a boy
16. Roosevelt's term for the word *fair*
17. Describes the Spanish-American War; opposite of long

Down

1. Roosevelt established new national parks, wildlife refuges, and national _____.
2. Under McKinley, Roosevelt was ____ president.
3. The Spanish-American was one.
5. Roosevelt learned to do this along with wrestling and hunting.
6. Islands next to Asia gained by the United States in the Spanish-American War
7. Roosevelt organized the _____ Riders.
9. Island whose demand for independence started the Spanish-American War
11. Roosevelt's nickname; used for a stuffed bear
14. Roosevelt helped settle a ____ strike.

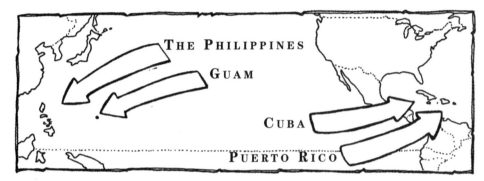

Land acquired by the United States in the Spanish-American War

Word List

box	forests	Rough	Teddy	war
coal	Philippines	short	trusts	York
Cuba	Puerto Rico	sickly	twentieth	youngest
	Pure	square	vice	

ANSWERS

Natives of North America, pages 6–7

European Explorers, pages 8–9

Colonial Life, pages 10–11

The Spanish Southwest, pages 12–13

Indians and Settlers, pages 14–15

The Colonists Protest, pages 16–17

The Revolutionary War, pages 18–19

Thomas Jefferson, pages 20–21

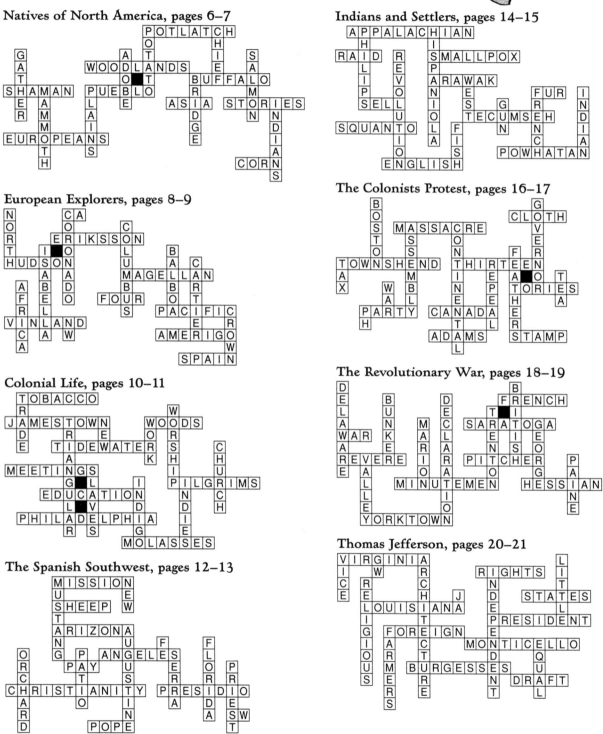

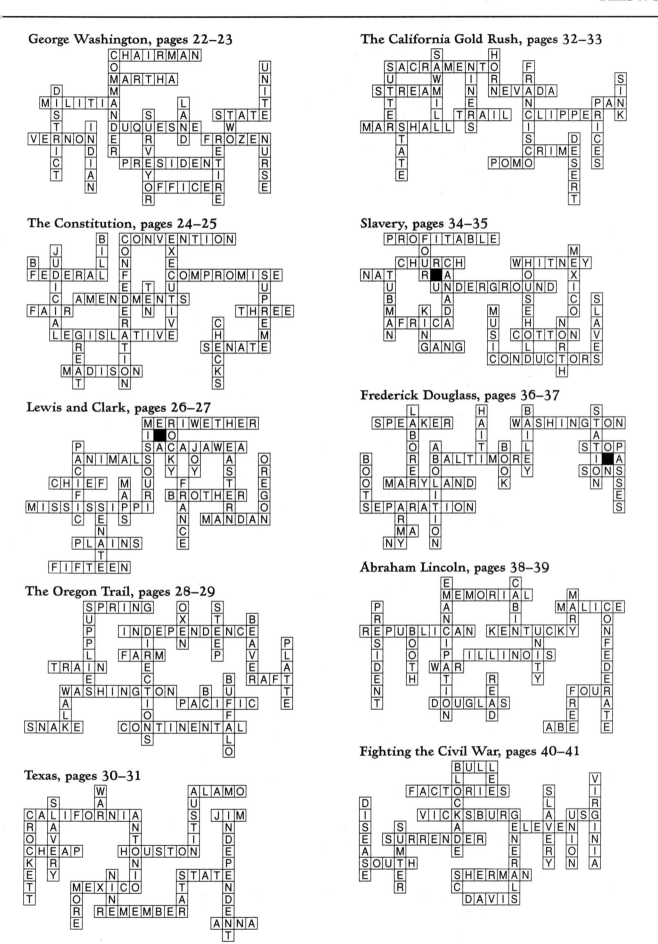

George Washington, pages 22–23

The California Gold Rush, pages 32–33

The Constitution, pages 24–25

Slavery, pages 34–35

Lewis and Clark, pages 26–27

Frederick Douglass, pages 36–37

The Oregon Trail, pages 28–29

Abraham Lincoln, pages 38–39

Fighting the Civil War, pages 40–41

Texas, pages 30–31

Answers

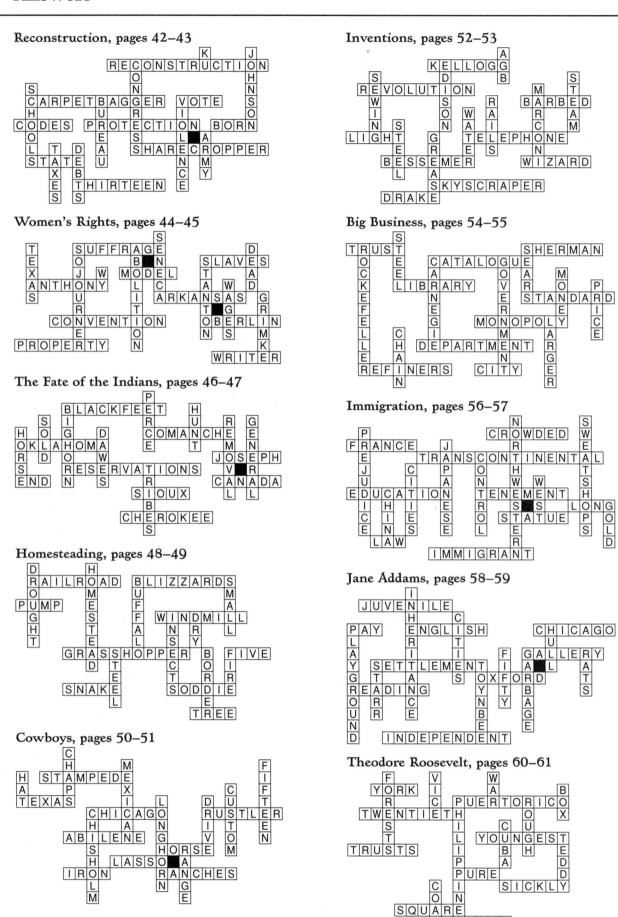

Reconstruction, pages 42–43

Women's Rights, pages 44–45

The Fate of the Indians, pages 46–47

Homesteading, pages 48–49

Cowboys, pages 50–51

Inventions, pages 52–53

Big Business, pages 54–55

Immigration, pages 56–57

Jane Addams, pages 58–59

Theodore Roosevelt, pages 60–61